Unma

Moms

Proof You're a Fantastic Parent Because There are
Mom Way Worse Than You.

A Parody

Written and Illustrated
By Selena Johnson

This Book Belongs to

_____

_____

In nursery room with baby's cry,
A new mom ponders with a sigh.
She's worried if she'll do what's right,
In long sleep-deprived, tiring nights.

In hallowed halls where cradles sway,
She ponders night and day,
With tender heart and trembling hands,
She faces fears the world demands.

Will I be good enough, she cries,
As moonlight dances in her eyes.
The cries of babes in tender years,
Whisper secrets to her ears.

Will I protect you from all harms,
Hold you ever in my arms?
Can I teach you right from wrong,
And sing you life's most wondrous song?

Her hands may shake, her heart may race,
With every little breath you take.
But through her worries, Fierce and wild,
She's bound to you, oh precious child.

In quiet rooms with soft night's glow,
She often wonders, minds in tow,

With hearts that beat in anxious race,
"What if" questions they must face.

"What if I'm not strong enough,
To guide through times both smooth
and rough?"

"What if in my tired daze,
I miss a step in motherhood's maze?"

"What if I cannot calm their cries,
Or sing the lullabies that dry the eyes?"

"What if I don't produce enough milk
To feed their growing needs?"

What if?...

But oh, dear mom, please understand,
That doubts and fears often go hand in hand,

You'll learn, you'll grow, you'll Find your way,
With each sunrise, a brand-new day.

For every "what if" that you bear,
Is but a testament that you care.

To Make it crystal Clear
You're a Way Better Mom Than Many.

No Matter how bad you think you are doing
You can't be anywhere close to these

animal Moms ...

Dolphin moms will keep their babies awake for a month straight after birth. Talk about sleep deprivation!

Hamster mothers are infamous for eating their babies if they're stressed. It's a far cry from a **comforting hug!**

If you feel guilty that you've served **mac 'n' cheese** for a week, re-member the **California Mouse** feeds their babies a diet of **faeces!**

When a **baby giraffe** is born, it's welcomed with a **six-foot** drop to the ground; talk about a rough start.

Momma giraffe doesn't believe in soft landings!

When they call you a **Screamer** and say that you're too loud, **Beagle moms** are known for howling or baying loudly, which can cause stress to their pups. It's not exactly a **lullaby!**

GoldFish moms are known to eat their own eggs after laying them.

It's an unexpected brunch menu!

Mama Bears are known to abandon or even **Consume** cubs if food resources are scarce. They prioritize their survival over their young.

If they call you a
pushover...

Some **Parakeet Moms** will push the weakest chick out of the nest, ensuring more resources for the stronger chicks.

When you feel bad for being a little late,

Mallard Moms will often lead their ducklings on marathon trips imme-diately after they hatch, some ducklings don't keep up.

Emperor Scorpion mothers may resort to eating their babies during times of stress or if conditions aren't right.

Budgie Moms lay more eggs than they can take care of and often neglect the youngest ones. Talk about

Overbooking!

If they accuse you of favouritism, Blue-footed booby mothers allow the stronger chick to kill its sibling. It's like an avian version of "Survivor"!

A **termite queen** can lay up to 30,000 eggs a day and let her offspring take care of them.
It's an assembly line of siblings!

Guinea Fowl moms will abandon their chicks at a very young age, forcing them to fend for themselves.

If you feel bad you've missed a school play due to work,

Harbor seal moms leave their pups alone on the beach often, exposing them to possible danger, while they go hunting. Seaside vacations can be hazardous!

often abandon slower ducklings during migration. It's survival of the Fittest!

Potbelly Pig moms will often roll over onto their piglets accidentally, leading to the demise of the unlucky ones.

It's a harsh reality in the pigsty!

When you're ashamed you forgot the Tooth Fairy...

Turkey moms often lose track of their poults and fail to notice if they stray or get left behind. Sounds like a headcount problem!

It's a literal jungle out there!

So...
When days are long and nights are tough,
And you feel you've had just enough,
Remember the critters in this tome,
And then glance around your nurturing home.

Unlike the scorpion, you don't chow down,
On your precious babes with a hungry frown.
You don't starve them or leave them like some creatures might,
You feed them love, not poop, day and night.

With each snuggle, and lullaby's zest,
Know in your heart, you're doing your best.
While wild moms may leave their kin to fate,
You build a haven, oh so great.

Through tears and laughter, through trials anew,
In tiny eyes, love is reflected back to you.
With each bandage, and every gentle word,
A warrior's spirit in your child is stirred.

So, to every mom, take a bow, take heart,
You're the life's anchor, an eternal work of art.
Take this trophy, hold it close and dear,
For you've achieved love's highest frontier.

Be proud, stand tall, through the storm you've sailed,
With love as your compass, you have prevailed.
In the tapestry of life, threaded with love's zest,

Always remember, **as a mom, you are the very best.**

The End

Printed in the USA
CPSIA information can be obtained
at www.ICGtesting.com
LVHW070028170923
758295LV00072B/1442